TYRANNOSAURUS REX

A Buddy Book
by
Richard M. Gaines

ABDO
Publishing Company

VISIT US AT

www.abdopub.com

Published by ABDO Publishing Company, 4940 Viking Drive, Edina, Minnesota
55435. Copyright © 2001 by Abdo Consulting Group, Inc. International copyrights
reserved in all countries. No part of this book may be reproduced in any form without
written permission from the publisher.

Printed in the United States.

Edited by: Christy DeVillier
Contributing editors: Mike Goecke, Matt Ray
Graphic Design: Denise Esner, Maria Hosley
Cover Art: Patrick O'Brien, title page
Interior Photos/Illustrations: pages 4, 6 & 7: ©1999-2001 Christopher Srnka; pages 8, 9
& 27: Corbis; pages 14 & 15: M. Shiraish ©1999 All rights reserved; page 15: Bruce E.
Shillinglaw; pages 16, 17 & 24: ©Douglas Henderson from *Living With Dinosaurs* by
Patricia Lauber, published by Bradbury Press; page 18: ©Douglas Henderson from
The Complete T-Rex, by Jack Horner & Don Lessem, published by Simon & Schuster;
page 21: Patrick O'Brien; page 23: Jodi Henderson.

Library of Congress Cataloging-in-Publication Data

Gaines, Richard, 1942-
    Tyrannosaurus rex/Richard M. Gaines.
        p. cm. – (Dinosaurs)
    Includes index.
    ISBN 1-57765-485-4
    1. Tyrannosaurus rex—Juvenile literature. [1. Tyrannosaurus rex. 2. Dinosaurs.] I.
Title.

QE862.S3 G37 2001
567.912'9—dc21

00-069984

TABLE OF CONTENTS

What Were They?....................................4

How Did They Move?..........................6

Why Was It Special? 8

Where Did They Live? 10

Land Of The T. Rex 12

Their Dinosaur Neighbors.................14

Who Else Lived There? 16

What Did They Eat? 18

Who Were Their Enemies? 20

Family Life 22

The Family Tree 24

Discovery 26

Where Are They Today?....................28

Fun Dinosaur Web Sites....................30

Important Words 31

Index 32

Tyrannosaurus rex
Tye-RAN-oh-SAWR-us recks
or T. rex

Tyrannosaurus rex means "terrible lizard king." This "king" dinosaur was one of the biggest, meat-eating animals ever. T. Rex was one of the smartest dinosaurs, too.

Tyrannosaurus rex was over 40 feet (12 m) long. That is about as long as a school bus.

Tyrannosaurus rex stood about 18 feet (6 m) tall. That is as tall as a giraffe.

An adult T. rex weighed about 10,000 pounds (4,536 kg). That is as heavy as two small elephants.

The T. rex had two strong arms. Each arm had two toes. These arms could lift 400 pounds (181 kg).

The T. rex's arms were three feet (one m) long. The T. rex could not touch its mouth with these arms.

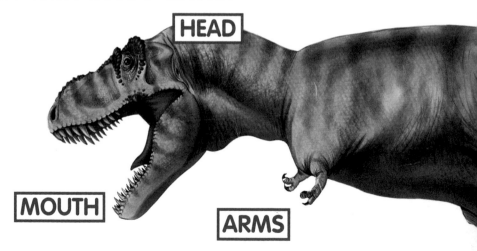

HEAD

MOUTH

ARMS

The Tyrannosaurus rex walked on two big legs. Its feet had three huge toes. Each toe was 50 inches (one m) long.

This giant dinosaur did not let its tail drag on the ground. It held the tail straight behind.

The T. rex was faster than most dinosaurs. It could run about 25 miles (40 km) per hour.

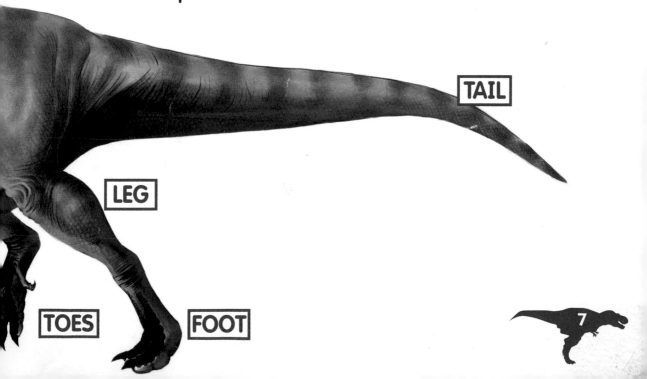

TAIL

LEG

TOES

FOOT

7

Paleontologist with a T. rex skull.

The Tyrannosaurus rex was a powerful eater. It could bite down very hard.

The T. rex had a special mouth for extra-large bites. It could eat 500 pounds (226 kg) of meat in one bite.

The T. rex's teeth were 6-12 inches (15-30 cm) long.

The T. rex did not chew its food. Instead, this mighty dinosaur swallowed whole chunks of meat and bone.

The T. rex had about 60 teeth. What happened if a tooth broke? Like sharks, the T. rex grew new teeth.

WHERE DID THEY LIVE?

The Tyrannosaurus rex lived in North America. North America looked very different 65 million years ago.

There used to be a sea in the western half of North America. This body of water was called the Colorado Sea. The T. rex lived on a chunk of land west of this Colorado Sea.

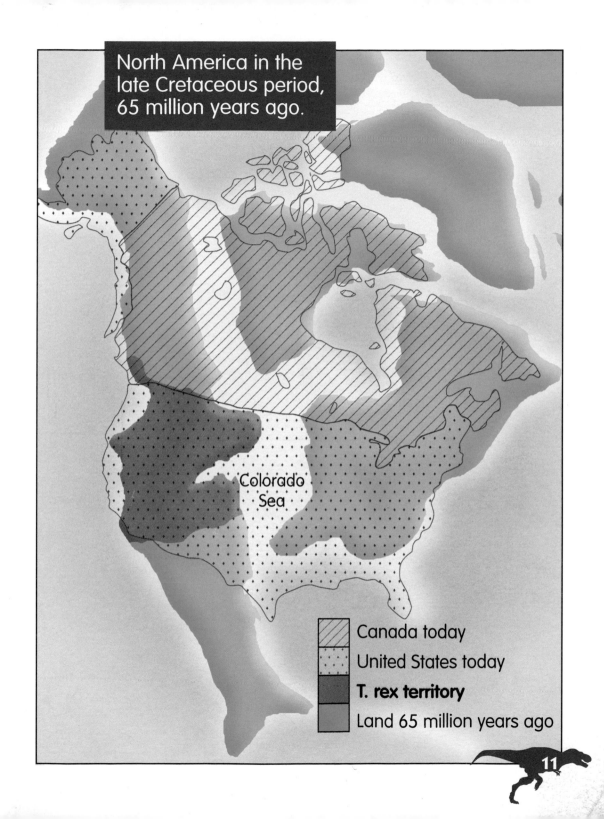

North America in the
late Cretaceous period,
65 million years ago.

Colorado
Sea

Canada today

United States today

T. rex territory

Land 65 million years ago

LAND OF THE T. REX

The T. rex lived in a very wet area. This area was full of lakes, streams, and mud. This is called a floodplain. The rivers that ran from the Rocky Mountains into the Colorado Sea created the floodplain.

The Florida Everglades is a floodplain.

Evergreen, or conifer, trees grew in the T. rex's environment. Flowering trees and plants, or angiosperms, grew there, too.

Flowering trees are angiosperms.

Angiosperms are the plants that make their seeds in flowers. These flowers grow fruit. The seeds are safe inside the fruit. Animals eat the fruit and spread the seeds throughout the forests. Magnolia, willow, oak, and apple trees are angiosperms.

Tyrannosaurus rex lived among the Hadrosaurs and the Ceratopsians. The Hadrosaurs were duck-billed dinosaurs. The Ceratopsians were dinosaurs with horns. Both the Hadrosaurs and the Ceratopsians were plant-eaters.

The Triceratops was a Ceratopsian. It had three horns on its head.

Triceratops

The Parasaurolophus was a Hadrosaur. It had a large hollow crest on the back of its head.

Parasaurolophus

The Maiasaura were Hadrosaurs, too. The Maiasaura built six-foot (two-m) nests in the mud of Montana. Like birds, they brought food to their young.

Maiasaura with their young.

15

The Tyrannosaurus rex lived among many mammals and birds.

The Hesperornis was a bird. It looked like a duck. But it had teeth in its beak. The Hesperornis spent most of its time in the water.

Hesperornis

Ichthyornis with a giant crocodile.

The Ichthyornis were birds, too. They looked like seagulls. Like the Hesperornis, the Ichthyornis had teeth. They could eat fish with these teeth. Ichthyornis means fish-bird.

Giant crocodiles, turtles, and frogs lived in the waters.

T. rex hunting for food.

The Tyrannosaurus rex was a meat-eater, or carnivore. This means it ate animals for food. Some paleontologists believe the T. rex hunted animals for dinner.

Other paleontologists think the T. rex ate animals it did not kill. This is called scavenging. Maybe the T. rex hunted and scavenged for food.

How much did the T. rex eat? A T. rex adult ate about 28,000 pounds (12,701 kg) of meat each year.

WHO WERE THEIR ENEMIES?

The mighty Tyrannosaurus rex did not have many enemies. The T. rex possibly fought each other. Maybe they battled over food, mates, and territory.

How did they fight? A Tyrannosaurus rex would gnaw with the side of his mouth. The T. rex could kick with his strong back legs, too.

Paleontologists believe T. rex did not often kill each other.

A battle between
T. rex and Triceratops.

FAMILY LIFE

How did T. rex mothers take care of their young? Some paleontologists believe a T. rex mother built nests. She would find a low spot on the ground. Then, she would fill this spot with rotting plants.

The T. rex mom would lay eggs in the nest. Then, she sorted the eggs so that they stood up. Birds allow their eggs to sit on their sides.

Eggs

The T. rex mother may have fed and guarded her young. But only until they were big enough to live alone.

Some paleontologists believe birds and crocodiles are related to dinosaurs. Crocodiles guard their eggs until they hatch.

THE FAMILY TREE

There are many dinosaurs related to the Tyrannosaurus rex. The early Tyrannosaurs lived in Thailand. Thailand is a country on the continent of Asia.

Some of the Tyrannosaurs spread to Africa and South America. Others migrated from Asia into North America across a land bridge.

Daspletosaurus

Did other Tyrannosaurs look like the T. rex? Yes, but there are some differences. For example, the Albertosaurus was smaller than the T. rex.

Another T. rex cousin is the Daspletosaurus. It was about the same size as the Albertosaurus. The Daspletosaurus had stronger arms than its cousins.

DISCOVERY

Have you heard of Sue? Sue is a Tyrannosaurus rex fossil.

Why is Sue important? This fossil is the most complete T. rex fossil ever found. Also, it is the best preserved, or saved.

Paleontologists learn a lot from well-preserved fossils. Paleontologists learned a lot from studying Sue.

Sue at the Field Museum in Chicago.

American Museum of Natural History
Central Park West at 79th Street
New York, NY 10024
www.amnh.org

Carnegie Museum of Natural History
4400 Forbes Avenue
Pittsburgh, PA 15213
www.clpgh.org/cmnh

Field Museum
1400 S. Lake Shore Drive
Chicago, IL 60605-2496
www.fieldmuseum.org/sue/default.htm

Royal Tyrrell Museum of Paleontology
Box 7500, Drumheller
Alberta T0J 0Y0 Canada
www.tyrrellmuseum.com

TYRANNOSAURUS REX

NAME MEANS	Tyrant Lizard King
DIET	Meat
WEIGHT	10,000 pounds (4,536 kg)
HEIGHT	18 feet (6 m)
TIME	Late Cretaceous Period
FAMILY	Theropod
SPECIAL FEATURE	Powerful bite
FOSSILS FOUND	USA—Colorado, Montana, South Dakota, Wyoming Canada—Alberta, Saskatchewan

T.rex lived 65 million years ago

First humans appeared 1.6 million years ago

Triassic Period	Jurassic Period	Cretaceous Period	Tertiary Period
245 Million years ago	208 Million years ago	144 Million years ago	65 Million years ago
Mesozoic Era			Cenozoic Era

29

Zoom Dinosaurs
www.EnchantedLearning.com/subjects/dinosaurs
Zoom Dinosaurs, designed for students of all ages, includes an illustrated dinosaur dictionary and classroom activities.

Walking with Dinosaurs
www.bbc.co.uk/dinosaurs
The British Broadcasting Company offers this fact-filled dinosaur site which features "Walking With Dinosaurs" interactive adventures.

Dinosaur Discovery Room
www.clpgh.org/cmnh/discovery
Presented by the Carnegie Museum of Natural History, this site invites children to learn about dinosaurs through detective games, riddles, and dinosaur jumbles.

IMPORTANT WORDS

carnivore a meat-eater.

conifer trees that have needles instead of leaves. Conifers stay green all year long.

continent one of the seven large land masses on earth.

Cretaceous period period of time that happened 144–65 million years ago.

dinosaur reptiles that lived on land 248-65 million years ago.

environment all of the animals and plants that live in a place.

floodplain a place that is flooded when a river overflows.

fossil remains of very old animals and plants. People commonly find fossils in the ground.

land bridge a small piece of land that binds two larger land areas.

mammals warm-blooded animals that feed milk to their young.

migrate to travel from one place to another, commonly to find food or mates.

paleontologist someone who studies very old life (like dinosaurs), mostly by studying fossils.

scavenger animals that eat dead animals that they did not kill themselves.

territory an exact area where a group of animals sleep and eat.

INDEX

Africa, **24**

Albertosaurus, **25**

angiosperm, **13**

Asia, **24**

carnivore, **18**

Ceratopsian, **14**

Colorado Sea, **10, 11, 12**

conifer, **13**

continent, **10, 24**

crocodile, **17, 23**

Daspletosaurus, **24, 25**

eggs, **22, 23**

floodplain, **12**

fossil, **26, 29**

Hadrosaur, **14, 15**

Hesperornis, **16, 17**

Ichthyornis, **17**

land bridge, **24**

Maiasaura, **15**

mammal, **16**

North America, **10, 11, 24,**

paleontologist, **8, 18, 19, 20,**
22, 23, 26

Parasaurolophus, **15**

plant-eater, **14**

scavenge, **19**

South America, **24**

Sue, **26, 27, 28**

territory, **11, 20**

Thailand, **24**

Triceratops, **14, 21**

Tyrannosaur, **25**